W9-CAJ-727

A TRUE BOOK™

UNDERSTANDING CLIMATE CHANGE

Facing a Warming World

Melissa McDaniel

Children's Press®
An Imprint of Scholastic Inc.

Content Consultants

Heidi A. Roop, PhD
Research Scientist
Climate Impacts Group
University of Washington, Seattle
Seattle, Washington

Farhana Sultana, PhD
Associate Professor of Geography
Maxwell School of Citizenship & Public Affairs
Syracuse University
Syracuse, New York

Library of Congress Cataloging-in-Publication Data

Names: McDaniel, Melissa, 1964– author.

Title: Facing a warming world/by Melissa McDaniel.

Other titles: True book.

Description: New York: Children's Press, an imprint of Scholastic Inc. 2020. | Series: A true book | Includes index. | Audience: Grades 4–6. | Summary: "The Book describes climate change and its effects on Society"—Provided by publisher.

Identifiers: LCCN 2019031413 | ISBN 9780531130780 (library binding) | ISBN 9780531133781 (paperback)

Subjects: LCSH: Climatic changes—Social aspects—Juvenile literature. | Climatic changes—Effect of human beings on—Juvenile literature. | Human ecology—Juvenile fiction.

Classification: LCC QC903.15 .M33 2020 | DDC 304.2/5—dc23

LC record available at https://lccn.loc.gov/2019031413

Design by THREE DOGS DESIGN LLC
Produced by Spooky Cheetah Press
Editorial development by Mara Grunbaum

Scholastic Inc., 557 Broadway, New York, NY 10012

1 2 3 4 5 6 7 8 9 10 R 29 28 27 26 25 24 23 22 21 20

Front cover: Kids join the fight against climate change.

Back cover: A student plants trees in Kenya.

Find the Truth!

Everything you are about to read is true *except* for one of the sentences on this page.

Which one is **TRUE**?

T or F   More than half of all electricity in the United States comes from wind power.

T or F   Solar energy costs about the same as energy from **fossil fuels**.

Find the answers in this book.

Contents

Millions of young people have taken part in climate marches.

Many cities now have charging stations for electric cars.

Engineering Earth

3 Climate Change and You

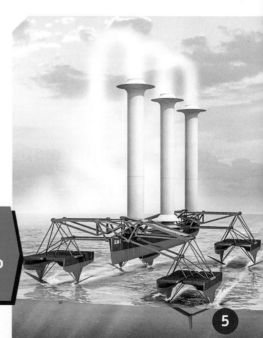

Researchers think "cloud brightening" technology might help slow climate change.

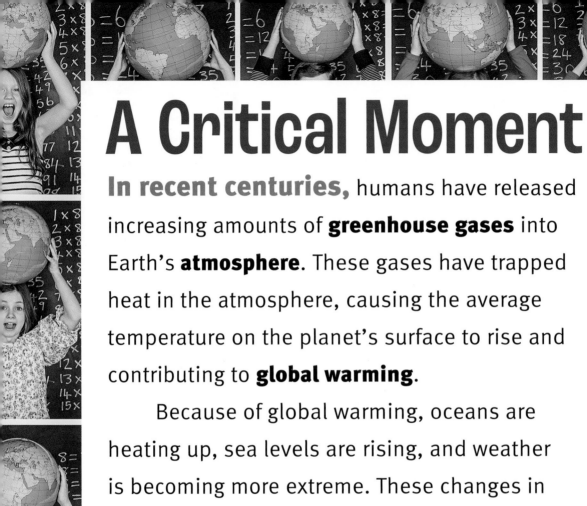

A Critical Moment

In recent centuries, humans have released increasing amounts of **greenhouse gases** into Earth's **atmosphere**. These gases have trapped heat in the atmosphere, causing the average temperature on the planet's surface to rise and contributing to **global warming**.

Because of global warming, oceans are heating up, sea levels are rising, and weather is becoming more extreme. These changes in Earth's climate are known as global **climate change**. They threaten people and other plant and animal species around the world. If we don't make changes to reduce greenhouse gas **emissions** now, these problems will worsen.

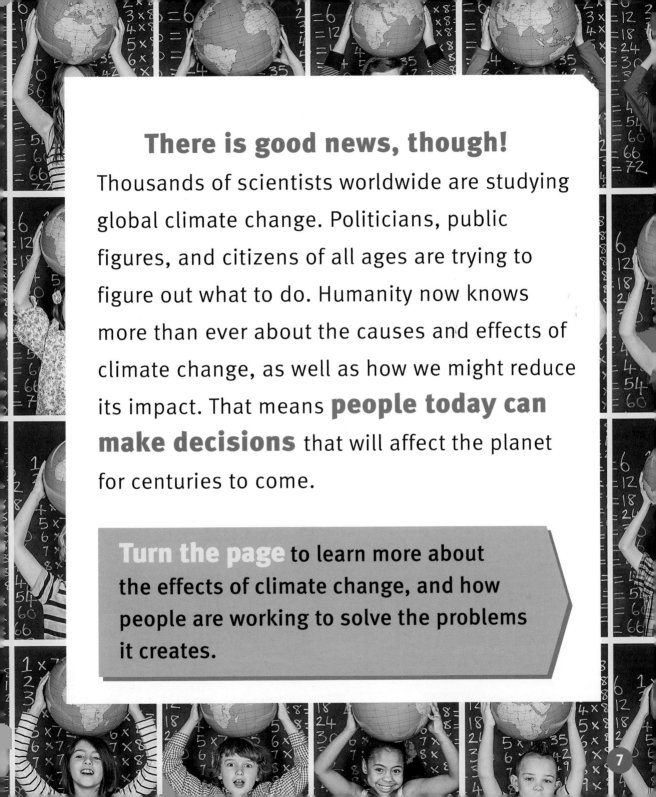

There is good news, though!

Thousands of scientists worldwide are studying global climate change. Politicians, public figures, and citizens of all ages are trying to figure out what to do. Humanity now knows more than ever about the causes and effects of climate change, as well as how we might reduce its impact. That means **people today can make decisions** that will affect the planet for centuries to come.

Turn the page to learn more about the effects of climate change, and how people are working to solve the problems it creates.

One of the most significant uses of coal is the production of electricity.

Coal-fired power plants account for about 30 percent of global carbon dioxide emissions.

The Dangers of Climate Change

Scientists first started to measure the effects of human activity on the climate in the mid-1800s. A century later, many scientists were alarmed about increasing pollution in the atmosphere. They noticed growing levels of **carbon dioxide**, a pollutant produced when people burn fossil fuels such as coal and oil. In time, the majority of scientists agreed that Earth is warming because of excess greenhouse gases, such as carbon dioxide, that are released by human activity.

Countries in Asia are most at risk from increased storms.

Dramatic Changes

Experts say that as of 2019, we have warmed the planet 1.8 degrees Fahrenheit (1 degree Celsius). And we are already seeing the effects of this warming around the globe. Because of the excessive heat, in some places the land dries out during long **droughts**. On the other hand, warmer air means more water evaporates, bringing more rain. That is why some areas around the world are experiencing more frequent and violent storms, as well as flooding.

Health Hazards

In 2019, many cities across Europe experienced the hottest temperatures ever observed there. Air-conditioning is rare in Europe. Without it, high temperatures can be dangerous, especially for people who are elderly. In some areas, "cool air shelters" now provide safe places for people when temperatures become too high.

The increased warmth is also expanding the range of insects that carry deadly diseases. For example, certain mosquitoes carry malaria, tsetse flies can cause a disease called sleeping sickness, and some deer ticks carry Lyme disease. With climate change, these diseases might become even more common.

Some mosquitoes pass on malaria if they have already bitten someone else who has the disease.

The ice in Antarctica and Greenland is melting.

Coasts at Risk

As Earth warms, **glaciers** and ice sheets melt, and sea levels rise. This endangers cities and villages built along the ocean. Rising sea levels could flood areas where millions of people live. Already some coastal towns and villages both in the United States and around the world have been relocated to higher ground. Recent research suggests that sea level rise will force 187 million people to move by 2050.

Nothing to Drink

Climate change is also threatening supplies of fresh water. When snow and ice on mountaintops melt in spring, fresh water runs into streams and lakes. That provides people with drinking water. But as Earth warms, less snow is building up in the winter, and glaciers are disappearing. Many glaciers along the Himalayas, in Asia, and in parts of South America and the American West are already losing their supplies of frozen water.

During a severe drought in Bolivia, in South America, water had to be trucked in.

Crops need sunshine and water to grow.

Food Shortages

Many effects of climate change put our food supply at risk. Droughts and storms can damage crops. Higher temperatures and changing rainfall patterns can also affect how well crops grow. In some places, as the climate changes, the amount of wheat, rice, and corn grown is expected to dramatically decline. Experts predict that food shortages will become more common.

Forced from Home

In 2006, a severe drought hit rural Syria in western Asia. Crops failed, and people went hungry. More than 800,000 people left the countryside. Those who fled, known as refugees, went to cities, seeking safety and support. But the cities were not able to handle all the newcomers. The turmoil helped fuel violent conflict across the nation. Some people were forced to leave the country.

Recent droughts in Syria have been the region's worst in 900 years.

A Syrian woman carries water in a refugee camp.

Too Smoky for School

Since climate change is making some areas hotter and drier, wildfires are becoming more common and more intense. And that is having serious effects on everyday life—beyond the loss of property.

The most destructive wildfire season ever recorded in California took place in 2018. Thousands of fires raced through the dry forests and grasslands. Smoke blew into cities and towns. Breathing smoke-filled air is bad for the lungs.

During the 2018 California fires, some people wore protective masks to keep from inhaling a lot of smoke.

Many schools had to cancel recess and other outdoor activities for days or weeks. In some places, school was shut down entirely until the fires could be controlled.

In 2013, workers in St. Louis, Missouri, built a floodgate to hold back overflow from the Mississippi River.

Uneven Effects

The effects of climate change do not affect everyone on the planet equally. Wealthier countries have more resources than developing countries do, so they can better adapt to the effects of climate change. For example, people who grow their own food suffer when drought kills their crops. Droughts have less impact on people who get food from many sources and on those who can afford to pay more to eat. As a consequence, poorer countries feel the effects of climate change more than others.

A worker stands on top of a wind turbine in Northern California.

In 2018, wind power supplied almost 14 percent of the electricity in the European Union, which covers most of Europe.

The World Responds

Scientists say that to slow climate change, people around the world will have to make major changes. One big step in the right direction is to reduce greenhouse gas emissions. Many countries and businesses around the world have started to take action to slow climate change.

Scientists in Antarctica collect snow for analysis.

Gathering Data

In 1988, the **United Nations** (UN) and the World Meteorological Organization (WMO) established the Intergovernmental Panel on Climate Change (IPCC). More than 190 countries signed on. Thousands of scientists around the world survey current research to provide accurate information on climate change. Using their findings, the IPCC projects how climate change will affect people and the environment in coming decades. Governments around the world use this information to set goals and make agreements about how to address climate change.

Kyoto Protocol

In 1997, countries around the globe adopted the Kyoto Protocol. A protocol is an agreement that sets rules. The Kyoto Protocol uses IPCC information to set targets for countries to reduce the greenhouse gases they send into the atmosphere. This was the first major international agreement of its kind. Almost every country has signed on to reduce their harmful emissions.

There are more than one billion cars, trucks, and buses on the world's roads.

The average car emits 5 tons (4.6 metric tons) of carbon dioxide every year.

Paris Agreement

In 2015, the Paris Agreement was adopted by nearly every nation in the world. The agreement aims to limit the increase in the average global temperature. Each country commits to cutting pollution and gets to decide how to help. The United States signed on in 2016. The next year President Donald Trump announced that the United States would withdraw from the agreement in 2020.

Nations Unies

Conférence sur les Changements Climatiques 2015

COP21/CMP11

Paris, France

World leaders celebrate the signing of the Paris Agreement.

Top 10 Carbon Dioxide Emitters

These ten countries produce the most carbon dioxide from burning fossil fuels:

1. China
2. United States
3. India
4. Russia
5. Japan
6. Germany
7. South Korea
8. Saudi Arabia
9. Canada
10. Iran

Source: https://www.cia.gov/library/publications/the-world-factbook/fields/274rank.html

Different Histories

European nations and the United States have been producing greenhouse gas emissions for a long time. They were the first to build factories, or industrialize. As other countries have developed in the same way, they too have produced more pollution. Today, China and the United States produce the most greenhouse gas emissions. As the United States continues to move manufacturing to other countries, the balance of pollution production continues to shift.

Making Important Changes

In addition to making treaties, the world's nations have responded to the challenge of climate change in different ways. Some countries have set aggressive targets for reducing greenhouse gases and are making changes quickly. For example, Sweden has committed to reducing greenhouse gas emissions to zero by the year 2045. Countries such as Costa Rica and Denmark have announced future bans on the sale of gasoline-powered cars.

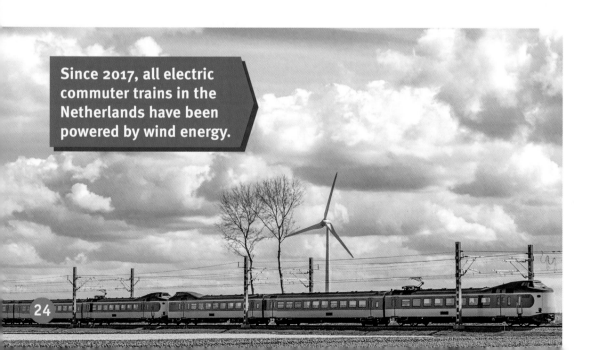

Since 2017, all electric commuter trains in the Netherlands have been powered by wind energy.

On the Road

Transportation, such as driving cars and trucks, burns fossil fuels and produces more greenhouse gas emissions in the United States than any other human activity. To cut pollutants, people need to reduce the number of gasoline-powered cars and trucks on the road. Driving fewer miles also decreases the amount of pollution sent into the atmosphere.

To reduce the release of greenhouse gases, Americans are increasingly buying cars powered by electricity rather than gasoline. Electric cars have batteries. Like phones, they need to be plugged in to be recharged.

Most electric cars can travel 200 miles (322 kilometers) before needing to be charged.

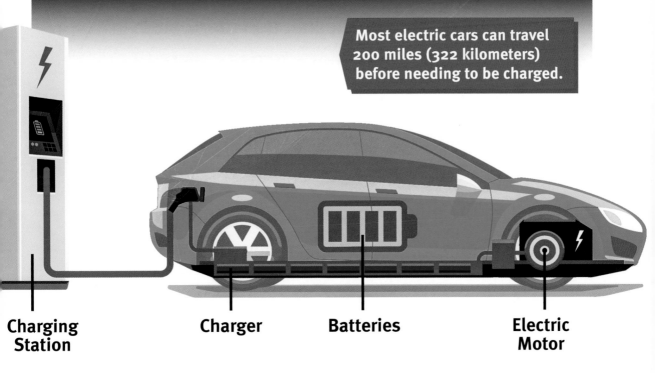

Charging Station

Charger

Batteries

Electric Motor

Geothermal energy uses heat from underground. It also creates heated pools and hot springs.

Cleaner Energy

Governments and businesses are also investing in energy sources that are cleaner and renewable. In other words, they do not run out. Renewable power comes from rivers, wind, sun, and even heat from underground. Those sources create hydroelectric, wind, solar, and geothermal energy, respectively. Almost all the electricity produced in Iceland, a country in northern Europe, is renewable.

Another carbon-free energy source is **nuclear power**. In France, more than 70 percent of electricity comes from nuclear energy.

Investing in Research

Some businesses and nations are responding to climate change by investing in research. They are working to come up with ways to produce electricity and to power vehicles without burning fossil fuels.

In the past, renewable energy such as solar and wind power cost much more than fossil fuel energy. But technology companies have invested in figuring out how to harness and store the power of the sun and the wind at a lower cost.

In the United States, the solar industry now employs twice as many people as the oil, natural gas, and coal industries combined.

Developing new technologies such as cost-effective solar panels can be expensive.

Success Stories

China has invested heavily in solar technology. That country is now manufacturing and using affordable, efficient solar panels. In the United States, the cost of solar energy dropped by almost 90 percent from 2009 to 2018. The technology for harnessing the energy of the wind has also improved. It has also become a reliable, readily available energy source. Solar and wind power now cost about the same as power from fossil fuels.

Timeline: Responses to Climate Change

1938: Scientists begin to understand how greenhouse gases affect climate.

1988: The Intergovernmental Panel on Climate Change is established.

1997: The Kyoto Protocol is adopted, setting targets for countries to reduce greenhouse gas emissions, effective in 2005.

Slow to Change

Despite these success stories, governments and businesses have sometimes resisted adopting greener policies. There are many reasons for this. For example, raising gasoline taxes might convince people to use their cars less. But the raising of taxes could make some drivers angry. People in the oil and coal industries might worry that the decrease in driving will cause them to lose their jobs. As a result, politicians might be reluctant to promote green policies because that could keep people from voting for them.

2010:
The first plug-in electric cars made for a wide U.S. market are released.

2015:
The Paris Agreement is adopted, prompting countries to create plans to limit greenhouse gases.

2018:
Renewable energy accounts for 17 percent of all electricity generated in the United States.

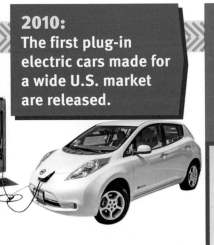

Nations Unies
Conférence sur les Changements Climatiques 2015
COP21/CMP11
Paris, France

Engineering Earth

Most experts agree that the most efficient way to slow climate change is by reducing the use of fossil fuels. But researchers are also considering other options. Some scientists are researching how to combat climate change by changing Earth's climate systems. This is called geoengineering. Let's look at some examples.

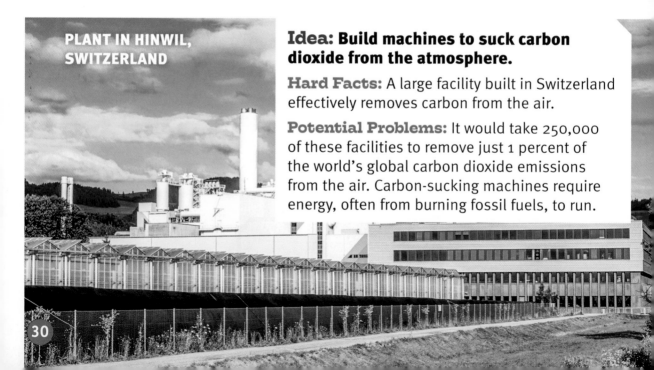

PLANT IN HINWIL, SWITZERLAND

Idea: Build machines to suck carbon dioxide from the atmosphere.

Hard Facts: A large facility built in Switzerland effectively removes carbon from the air.

Potential Problems: It would take 250,000 of these facilities to remove just 1 percent of the world's global carbon dioxide emissions from the air. Carbon-sucking machines require energy, often from burning fossil fuels, to run.

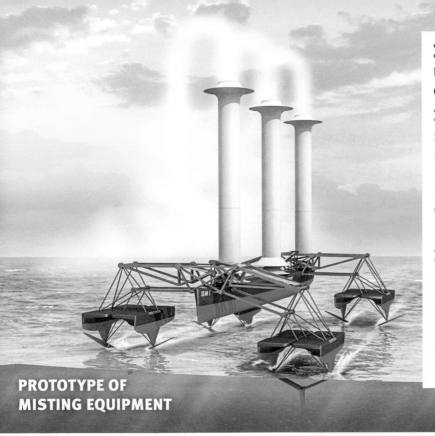

Idea: Add seawater mist to clouds over the oceans to brighten them.

Hard Facts: Light surfaces reflect more sunlight than dark ones. Brighter clouds will reflect some of the sun's light, which warms Earth, back into space.

Potential Problems: It might be difficult to produce enough mist to make a difference, and the misting equipment would need to withstand extreme weather and ocean conditions.

PROTOTYPE OF MISTING EQUIPMENT

Idea: Send millions of small mirrors into orbit around Earth.

Hard Facts: The mirrors would have to block only a small amount of sunlight to have a large effect on global warming.

Potential Problems: Launching the mirrors would be expensive. Some mirrors would not stay in orbit, so they would require constant maintenance.

PROTOTYPE OF ORBITAL SOLAR FARM

On July 14, 2019, the temperature in northern Canada reached 69.8°F (21°C), the highest ever recorded.

The breaking up of sea ice is a natural, seasonal occurrence.

Climate Change and You

Many people find it difficult to imagine the real effects of climate change. In part, this is because the effects can be gradual. In recent decades, sea level has risen an average of one-tenth of an inch per year. But that small, regular increase makes a big difference over time. Understanding the future effects of climate change means thinking 10, 50, or even 100 years ahead.

What Is Normal?

It can be hard to understand climate change without knowing what is "normal" for an environment. For example, thousands of different kinds of creatures live in coral reefs. The reefs are fragile and easily affected by changes in their environment. Imagine that you are swimming along a reef. You might be very excited to see 20 brightly colored fish nearby. But you might not know that just a few years earlier, thousands of fish swam in the same spot. What is considered "normal" today has changed.

Warming ocean temperatures can kill coral reefs.

From Sad to Motivated

The size of the problem of climate change can seem overwhelming. Thinking about it can make people feel sad, scared,

Thousands of students in Portugal joined the SchoolStrike4Climate global protest in March 2019.

or powerless. For some people, it is hard to imagine a happy future. They wonder: Can we make a difference? Other people react differently. They use the predictions about the warming world as motivation to start working to help solve the problem. People throughout the world have already started movements to initiate change.

What Can You Do?

There are many lifestyle changes people can make to combat climate change. For example, you can walk, ride a bike, or use public transportation whenever you can rather than riding in a car.

Some people have stopped eating beef and dairy products in an effort to help the planet. The way cows digest food leads to an increase in methane emissions, and methane is a powerful greenhouse gas. If beef consumption decreases, fewer cows will need to be raised.

A study showed that meat and dairy farms produce 60 percent of agriculture's greenhouse gas emissions.

Avoiding throwaway plastic products helps cut down on carbon emissions.

Students from Kenya planted mangrove trees to help stop erosion.

To be part of a larger movement, you can join protests. You can create signs and join marches to raise awareness and urge politicians to act.

Planting trees in a yard, in a neighborhood, or in forests that have been burned by wildfires is also a great way to help. Planting trees combats climate change because trees remove carbon dioxide from the atmosphere. They also help protect coastlines from storms. There are many things people are doing to combat climate change. You need to decide what is right for you.

Global Changes

People in all parts of the world are coming up with smart ways to limit the damage from climate change. Farmers in the American Midwest are working to prevent their land from eroding, or wearing away, during floods. Some are planting cover crops to keep the soil in place in winter after food crops have been harvested.

Much of the Netherlands lies below sea level. To prevent floods, people have built tall gates on a canal that leads to the city of Rotterdam.

Floodgates collect floodwater and direct it into lakes and parks.

Fighting for the Future

According to the IPCC, we need to limit Earth's temperature increase to no more than 2.7°F (1.5°C) to prevent the most disastrous effects of climate change. This will require real effort by people around the globe. Kids all over the world have been carrying protest signs with a simple message that says it all: "There is no Planet B." We live on a one-of-a-kind Earth, and it is up to us to preserve our planet and protect it for future generations. 🌍

How Climate Change Is Viewed

Scientists collect information on how the climate is changing. They also collect data about people's views of climate change. They ask people questions, such as how much of a problem they think the warming world is, and how much of a problem they think it will be in the future. These questions are important because how people think about climate change affects how the government responds to it.

The graph at the right shows how Americans' views of the risks of climate change have changed over time. Study the graph, and then answer the questions.

Americans' Views on the Risk of Climate Change

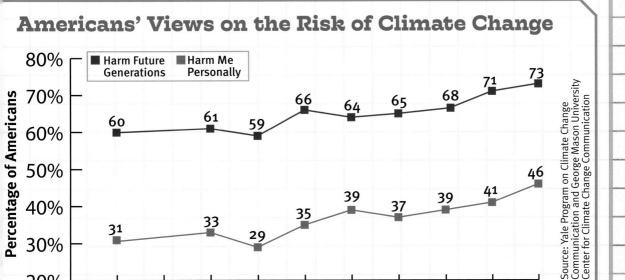

Source: Yale Program on Climate Change Communication and George Mason University Center for Climate Change Communication

Analyze It!

1. In 2008, what percentage of Americans believed that future generations would be harmed by climate change?

2. In 2017, Americans' belief that climate change would affect them personally had changed how much since 2008?

3. In 2017, how much higher was the percentage of people who worried about the risk of climate change on future generations than about the harm that would come to themselves? Think about what you've read in this book. Why do you think people were more worried about future generations?

Leading the Way

In 2018, Greta Thunberg, a 15-year-old girl from Stockholm, Sweden, was growing frustrated with her government's lack of action on climate change. To bring attention to the problem, she began a school strike for climate in her home city. Each Friday, instead of going to school, she protested in front of government buildings.

Greta Thunberg has inspired millions of people around the world, including these in Australia, to join her Fridays for Future strikes.

Over time, that attention arrived. Many people posted pictures of Thunberg on social media, and reporters interviewed her. Thunberg's message about the need to act spread. She became famous worldwide.

Thunberg's strikes and her message inspired millions of students in other countries to strike. More than seven million people took part in a global climate strike in September 2019.

Thunberg also drew the attention of politicians. She gave speeches at the European Parliament and at the United Nations Climate Action Summit. She accused adults of stealing the future from young people by not dealing with climate change. Many politicians became aware of the implications of climate change because of the actions of Thunberg and other young people.

True Statistics

Percentage of electricity produced in the United States from nuclear energy: 20

Percentage of electricity produced in France from nuclear energy: 72

Percentage of electricity produced in the United States from renewable sources: 17

Percentage of electricity produced in Iceland from renewable sources: 100

Number of gasoline-powered cars on the road in the United States in 2018: 276 million

Number of plug-in electric cars on the road in the United States in 2018: 1 million

Increase in average sea level since the start of the 20th century: 8 inches (20 cm)

Number of trees planted in Ethiopia in one day in 2019 to help combat climate change: 350 million

Did you find the truth?

(F) **More than half of all electricity in the United States comes from wind power.**

(T) **Solar energy costs about the same as energy from fossil fuels.**

Resources

Other books in this series:

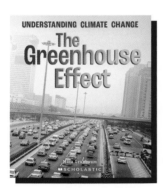

You can also look at:

Eschbach, Christina. *Inside Electric Cars*. North Mankato, MN: Core Library, 2019.

Sneideman, Joshua, and Erin Twamley. *Climate Change: Discover How It Impacts Spaceship Earth*. White River Junction, VT: Nomad Press, 2015.

Sneideman, Joshua, and Erin Twamley. *Renewable Energy: Discover the Fuel of the Future With 20 Projects*. White River Junction, VT: Nomad Press, 2016.

Thunberg, Greta. *No One Is Too Small to Make a Difference*. New York: Penguin, 2019.

Glossary

atmosphere (AT-muhs-feer) the mixture of gases that surrounds a planet

carbon dioxide (KAHR-bun dye-AHK-side) a gas that is a mixture of carbon and oxygen, with no color or odor

climate change (KLYE-mit chaynj) global warming and other changes in the weather and weather patterns that are happening because of human activity

droughts (drouts) long periods of time without rain

emissions (ih-MISH-uhnz) substances released into the atmosphere

fossil fuels (FAH-suhl FYOO-uhlz) coal, oil, and natural gas, formed from the remains of prehistoric plants and animals

glaciers (GLAY-shurz) slow-moving masses of ice found in mountain valleys or polar regions. A glacier is formed when snow falls and does not melt because the temperature remains below freezing.

global warming (GLOW-buhl WAR-ming) the rise in temperature around Earth due to heat from the sun trapped by greenhouse gases in the atmosphere

greenhouse gases (GREEN-hous GAS-ez) gases such as carbon dioxide and methane that contribute to the greenhouse effect

nuclear power (NOO-klee-ur POU-ur) power created by splitting atoms

United Nations (you-NIGH-ted NAY-shuns) a group of countries banded together to promote peace, security, and international cooperation

Index

Page numbers in **bold** indicate illustrations.

About the Author

Melissa McDaniel is a writer and editor living in New York City. She is the author of more than 30 books for young people. She has also written for the American Museum of Natural History, the Wildlife Conservation Society, and National Geographic Online. Melissa considers climate change the most urgent issue of our time. But she also believes that solutions are available and that, with effort, the necessary changes can be made to secure the future of the planet.